CROSSING
THE LINE

Andrey Gritsman

Červená Barva Press
Somerville, Massachusetts

Červená Barva Press
USPS P. O. Box 53
Somerville, MA 02143

editor@cervenabarvapress.com
http://www.cervenabarvapress.com

Visit the bookstore at:
http://www.thelostbookshelf.com

Production: Allison O'Keefe

Cover design: Asya Dodina
The cover features the work by Asya Dodina and Slava Polishchuk
Exit XVIII from the Exits and Corners series.

Copyright @ Asya Dodina, Slava Polishchuk

ISBN: 978-1-950063-87-1
LCCN: 2025941721

CONTENTS

I

II

CROSSING THE LINE

I

CROSSING THE LINE

The world was glistening inside my soft universe
in the filigreed web of warmth,
pulsating and feeding my unborn hopes,
tentacles of attachments, frustrations, death.

I could have been a father, a sister,
carpenter, savior, the judge, an executioner.
My actuarial survival
was not yet registered.
The winds of unknowing
caressed my mother's skin.
And the pain was vanishing

because I did not exist anymore.
I was not accounted for.
And still, brothers and sisters,
we were bonded and floating together
in the shared hardship.
For only you could appreciate
my gift to you:
my silent grace, the gentle beauty, dignity
and what I would not have done to the world.

And remember, there are others
for whom not only I
but also you
are a mistake.

CHANGE OF SCENERY

It's dead. Dead now.
Gray morning landscape still.
Last time I passed here
there was flickering of life,
pulsating creek
by the main road.
Now - images motionless,
like passion boxed
into a digital gallery.

I don't owe her anything
anymore. Not a sigh. Nothing left.
Our former home stained
with somebody else's breath.
Empty for the day, with stale bread
on the plastic kitchen table.
Only poplar in the backyard
still the same, with withered
cat scratches.

It is strange, how soul vision
changes the scenery.
No way back and soul
slowly awakens, looking
for a new home. Homes
and oak trees detached
and only sound of the train
shore bound reminds me
of distant destinations,
warm spots on the backdrop
of dead winter beauty.

ESCAPE

There are moments in life
and in history when *escape*
rhymes with *destiny*.
Alone, however, doesn't rhyme
with *lonely*, but *love* goes along
with *leave*. So, my long-distance,
long-term, long-gone interlocutor:
great souls destined
to escape demons of madness
and idiocy, two bloodless Siamese,
who play cards
in the train that rattles to the dead
end in a no-man's-land full of
the broken limbs and so-familiar
formalin jars with brains and hearts.
But we just jumped the train
ahead of schedule, on time,
in the only destined station,
in our case paradoxically set
in the midst of the imperial,
pompous, dead exuberance.

FAREWELL

We are standing with a group of strangers
at predawn hour by the unpaved road waiting
for our ride. Three hours to the station.

The lake is still asleep—splash of the paddle:
lonely fisherman adds his brushstroke
to the night's lunar landscape.

I am eight, holding hands
with my grandparents and the flock of wild ducks
above us is streaming away, like our destinies,
into a bottomless well of the full moon.

WHITE LIES

I live my life by white lies.
And poetry is white lies.
Second language is white lies also.
As well as the first.
But language is the only way
to hide love.
White, black, transparent
Or otherwise invisible.
So, all day long,
All life long I say white lies
To hide my love. In fact
I never know to whom.
It may be to you
But if I say it it would be a white lie.
But once it is said in a poem
It stays and as a bird flies away
In search of it's destiny.

TUNNEL

Don't remember my last words
at the daybreak, when the highway
runs beyond the cliff,
through the swamp to the hills,
where weathered flag
flaps under bare sky.

There was no real farewell,
no forgiveness. What's left—
coins in my pockets for
unanswered calls in to space.

There is no echo, but
the sound of a distant siren.
Flicker of taillights,
cars diving into the tunnel
underneath frozen river—
lights disappearing.

TWO PLANES

Two lines from the planes on the sky.
Two parallel flights who knows where.
Two souls lost in the world,
asleep on the planes by the window.

They dream their lines converge.
No matter where, in mirrored faraway.
When they passed customs
turn around and together
come out to town lightly
and disappeared.

TWO STONES

for M.D.

Two stones
on two distant coasts.
Coastal life variable, escaping.
Steel light in the morning
hint of moss in the air.
Smell of distant fisheries
abandoned.
Seven potato dishes on the menu.
All is not what it seems.
We both know that—
occupational malaise.

I lost you as we lose
everything eventually moving away
into the open sea,
seemingly motionless
from the distance,
passing through nobody's waters,
no knowledge predicted.
Love, still barely visible
far away, the only
thing real
in the primordial chaos.

GLIMPSE

Unseasonably warm. End of the world,
At least the way we know it?
The end of the road. The road washes out
In the spring. Dead foliage, touched by
The frost. Fireworks on the Mountain.
Fragments falling down, extinguished,
Down to the clearing, where once
She dropped her glove from the chairlift
Going up the mountain. There
The fireworks twice a year remind me
Of July, of the last words that we still
Were saying to each other
As one live organism. Nothing serious, just
That winters had been getting unseasonably warm.

UNSELTERING SKY

It was hard to believe:
Life's outgrown the legend,
time has eclipsed,
space has come to an end,
Gibraltar turned Atlantis,
wind and a desert merged
into one sky.

Coffee cup, and oriental rug,
mint tea sippers on the dusty veranda,
watching the quarterfinals
on the black and white
TV through suffocating
cigarette smoke,
dirty green waves on the horizon
reading Homer.

Snapshots, colored
fragments of commonplace
that will disappear
in someone's chest.
He was a landscape himself,
shadow crossed Central Park,
leaving trace in the snow,
in the sand.

Lonely traveler, his death
became new language,
poetry turned
into a palpable matter,
breathable air itself.

COLLOSSEUM

Geometry of death. Sun-blasted oval,
sandblasted stone.
Stale bread,
a song of wind
long gone to the groves
of memory.
Interlacement, entwinement
on the twilight
of the valley.
A tourist trap by day,
cemetery of stone
at night.

Now we know:
salt on the soil of Carthage,
salt beneath Masada,
they had sailed on the sails
toward nothingness
of the bloodhounds
of dead Caesars
to the dead end.

We float on the somnolent siesta
of Italian shadows
in the courtyard:
pasta is fresh, sauce
of the ancient recipe,
like sun, blasting impartially,
blissfully, melting makeup
on the mask of a face
of a lively tour guide
of the Berber origin.

RAIN JAZZ

Raindrops drum their jazz on Monday.
Universe of sleet. Unnamed motels,
Surplus warehouses, shut down stations,
Convenience stores drowned
in the ravines of suburban oblivion.

What comes to mind to the souls
sealed in their autos, not gone mad yet,
not turning left.

It's a good time to rethink life
from left to right.
If only I could return
to that city of elm-trees
for the sleepy summer.

I maybe the last one, who believes
that time is innocent and the school
opens its doors one day
to let me in
for the time
being.
I am gone for a week
till next Monday,
but find myself in a sheetrock motel
flat on nobody's bed,
chain on the door.

Jazz of rain plays its theme
on window pane.
Truck roars on the ramp.
I am trying to make sense of this all
in the sealed room, feeling
it's time to get up
and get lost like Tolstoy.
Leave into the starry night
through the door
thrown open.

But, if you leave – no return,
not for a time.
No exit for the time being.

MOTEL

All cheap motels possess
that terrible smell of dispossession,
dislodgement, airless sleep, and plastic crucifixion,
an owlish, shapeless face
behind the double-glass window,
the smell of life unlived,
of old rugs and dusty sorrow.

What can be dimmer than
the night of dreams that followed
the thick, tenacious odor
of the sleepy hollow.

You leave behind
this street and a frozen meadow,
the only blinking light.
You leave behind
a vacant cube of the borrowed,
of the sealed, stale, and silent space,
where one stays overnight,

where time is seized,
the pool is dry and cracked,
the phone is dead,
TV black and white,
the corner pizza place closed
last winter
and the street sign says: Do Not Enter.

II

BOAT

For Yu. G.

There is a wooden shed by the Moscow Presnya subway station,
a Georgian eatery where my friend is served
the best dumplings. He is in the back room next to the dusty ficus
by the kitchen door.
This used to be a local community club
where Brezhnev's portrait hung on a dilapidated wall.

My friend downs a shot of vodka, topped by sparkling water,
wolfs down stuff on his plate,
but thoughtfully. He remembers the misty Hudson,
us together on the Circle Line, passing
through summer, by piers and parks,
by a restricted area,
listening to the Indian song of Canadian winds.

I am sitting at the river café, having
penne arrabiatta, drinking Valpolichella,
looking at the same boat
that is heading toward our meeting point,
always there.

Dust floats from the Metro-North tracks.
Here you can get real close to the river.
On the opposite side is the Park Police Headquarters.

It's nobody's business how we throw our words, and they fly away
on northerly winds.
That's how poems are. This is our meter.

So from a distance we are both looking at the boat,
into our plates, at the sky;
I look at my Caesar salad, my friend at his dumplings.

Manhattan floats to Canada as the Flying Dutchman
to our meeting point,
God knows where,
where our words freeze in flight,

lit by unreachable light
in the boundless, echoing, Arctic space.
We are not there yet,
since our words are
still flying.

HUDSON

Discount rate is over.
Snow packed.
It's time for Nature's
farewell to life.
Ice-frozen milk—live pearl.
I'm off for a walk.
Somewhere a child is born,
talkative, naive.

I have one last miraculous
word to say.
Stop by the post office,
Flag flattering
in the Canadian wind.
In fifty yards—little store,
overlooking the river,
abandoned, windows boarded.

The owner, old
Marine veteran, gone
last summer. I'd walk up
next door to my beloved shop:
local treasures, crafts and stones,
to find her a necklace, bracelet,
and a ring—for my beloved,
I haven't met.

EMPTY HOUSE BY HUDSON

House by rocky stream abandoned,
even traces of souls evaporated.
Shrubs overgrown, gate broken.
Glacier erratics silent.
No one will die there anymore.
Nobody prepares the bed.
I am just a passerby,
incidental traveler.
I am calm, my return
secured. For some reason
my soul's in the empty house.
It calls me to come back
to the dark corners, to dust.
This is my regular stroll,
passing the house,
passing myself
on the road unknown.

GERMAN RUG

Captured rug.
Milk stain.
I am five, sore throat.
Light stain of Soviet champagne.
My father's young, 1955 New Years?
The rug's eternal, sturdy German job.
Deep in the texture—
traces of the German family:
Brandenburg, Silesia.
Along the advance of the 33rd army,
3rd Belorussian front.
Now we are relatives with
an unknown, untraceable family.
Captured rug.

LIGHT IN THE CATHEDRAL

Light from nowhere to nowhere.
Wreck of statues on the tiled floor.
Dark crypt is empty.
Judas silent in the corner.
And He is invisible in the chapel,
there is cold and echo of emptiness.
There is nobody to wait for.
Crosses deserted in the dusk.
Still light fell on the floor reveals
the fragments of the marble dream.
Cathedral under repair.
Shadows. And you and I
are alone there.

BUST

I turned on Channel 20
in the faceless, plastic hotel room.
Real-time story, documentary,
Johns bust,
soliciting, you know...

Curvy, drop-dead Latina female officer
posed as a hooker:
miniskirt, long boots, big bust,
patrolled the corner
by the pharmacy as
the GM SUV stopped,
window opened.
She leaned, exposed her
barely-hidden treasure,
and they got him!

He slowly stepped out, limping.
Walking with a cane, bald head,
older man, face invisible,
legally-required digital spot
blurred his face
on the TV screen.

Three muscular cops holding him
had a hard time putting on the cuffs:
the cane, probably bad back.
He could not bend backward
and twist his arms.
He was led away
into the police van for booking.

Gorgeous Latina added lipstick
to her plump lips.
The back-up crew took position
behind the Wal-Mart truck,
watching their bait.

I switched to the History Channel
and watched for a while
American GIs advancing in the jungle,
and Captain Franklin P. Eller
talking on the field phone
held by the South Vietnamese serviceman
during the Tet Offensive.

Then I fell asleep
before tomorrow's early meeting,
before the quick omelet in the coffee shop downstairs
with unforgettable sunny Polish waitress Renata,
who has not passed her exams yet
and was stuck in the joint,
hopefully not for long.

DEAD AIR

Static and dead air
on incoming calls.
You will experience
silence while you are waiting
for the next available
operator. Your call may be
monitored for quality
assurance purposes,
unless dead and static air
interferes with your
communication.
Anything incoming
may not be transmitted
due to current conditions.

In the meantime,
please, be aware
that proper entities
are working to restore
favorable conditions.
Be advised to be alert
and prepared for immediate
change of circumstances.
All assigned personnel
should remain at their
present locations and await
further instructions.
All nonessential personnel
should proceed to the designated
areas, avoiding static and dead air
at all costs.

FORGET THE WEDDING

Forget the wedding, but all will be ground into flour.
Endless flakes are behind the glass,
as if the airy mill in the sky
flung open its corn bins.

Somehow the snow is unseasonably early.
And then I tell myself
that fresh wounds will heal
by November or December, by January.

Well, I will leave, and all
will be resolved: time heals, the road is easy.
Perhaps I will visit myself—after all, it's abroad.
My hand will not tremble,
having shown the deep blue passport
to the girl in uniform.
Yes, that's it, a citizen of the USA.
The legs feed the wolf for the time being,
and I will rest, having sat down
before the road, in transit, by the counter, by the bar,
only there to find myself
before boarding, and there is still time
to look at the visa stamps
in the passport, its photo contains someone's
disturbed eyes—as if a stranger's.

We carelessly passed one another,
but our souls did not exchange
a single word. This is the way it should be:
close the door without sadness,
release the soul into the wind,
like a bird from the Garden of Eden.

SIEGE OF MOSCOW

General Guderian touched his moustache,
fixed binoculars on his trench coat.
Noticed first snowflake over burnt out field.
This is beginning of the end – thought General.
A shell flew over to the invisible target.
General unfolded large scale plan:
Alexandrov, Vyazma, Chimki, Moscow.
Cold rains, winter is close.
Deadly large fishes float slowly in the sky.
Everything is frozen: field, forest, the lake.
And on the old photo Guderian himself is frozen in dead calm.
Sky is graying, Winter is closer.
Snowflakes descend slowly on the wasteland –
as blind agents
from the near and faraway
renamed lands.

LAST WORDS

Unseasonably warm. End of the world,
at least the way we know it.
The end of the road. The road washes out
in the spring. Dead foliage, untouched by
the night frost. Fireworks on the mountain.
Fragments falling down, extinguished.
Down to the clearing, where once
you dropped your glove from the chairlift.
Going to the top. There,
the fireworks remind me
of July, of the last words we were still
saying to each other
as one live organism. Nothing serious, just
that winters had been getting
unseasonably warm.

LOCKDOWN

Rainy season lingers and lingers.
Fences all wet.
Out of town: shops, warehouses, barns
all grey and damp, gas stations sullen.
Long freight train still and merged into
landscape, as well as railway barrier.
We locked in our cars, fall into deep sleep.
Who knows when the city is open again.
There, probably, nobody's laughing or crying,
Just waiting for the second coming.
Which is not happening. This season
lingers for three generations. All is
wet and damp: churches, prisons and
hamlets. Nobody knows when is the wake up call.
That's how we live now. Everyone is his own savior.
And still we see the mirage on the horizon.
There faraway in the vanishing light
one can discern Kinneret on the contour map.

METRO-NORTH

Chelsea—Manchester United.
He is on the corner sofa.
Roasted chicken from the Tops,
German-style potato salad,
Heineken Light.
Chelsea—an accidental goal
served from the corner.
Abramovich will sack
the manager again—he thinks.
She is in the city.
Way back—in the motel
by LaGuardia with her lover,
then lunch at the Sheraton.
Now—boutiques in Soho.
Dead calm. He thinks:
Time to treat the porch.
Overtime, one more
Heineken. Calls her
again and again. Phone's
in the car. She remembers:
Pick up Lopressor for him,
Blahnik before close.
Leaves grow rusty.
Emerald mornings.
Echo from Metro-North
dying in crisp
autumn air.
Dying on the way
to the invisible island.

MOSCOW WALK

There is nothing left.
Still flows snowfall of the poplar fur.
A couple of watering holes.
The tram's end station beyond the city line.
Soccer dust in overgrown courtyards.
What else? Thank God it's still there.
Then who'll understand, who'll remember, who'll turn sad?
Childhood, youth sailed away.
A dovecote burned down, broken memory thread.
And the cold scales cover the dead plastic of the Fourth Rome.
Nothing's left,
And who will grasp—
this white city is covered with the tight net
of the security watch.
Still, my free memory walks along
Moscow Boulevard Ring.
But the dark raven follows me, unnoticed
in the twilight.

NIGHT WATCHMAN

Only rusty railroad tracks
beyond this point.
Train has gone deep
into the woods.
Wheels turn slowly, slower.
They will seize turning
without a trace.
There, in the words,
only night wind rustles.
No thunder, no sunrise,
only gray milk.
Maybe we are left
with just one night
together.

Let's bring out
our snack to a quiet place.
Say, by the river,
or by the ravine where
something flickers
and rustles.
The night watchman will not appear
anymore as the cloud of dust
or column of fire.
Just will turn soundlessly
into a willow tree.

N.J. STATE HIGHWAY

The strips of dead, fluorescent life
stream sightlessly away.
They shed the cold and crackling light
along the state highway.

The moaning curvatures of turns
are the only ones to call
for anyone. The roadside malls
are the spaces of no recall.

Eternity of the empty stores
is sealed by a concrete wall.
There hangs above the parking lot
the lunar, dim eyeball.

Gas stations are the only nests
of alienated warmth,
where Poles, Chicanos, and Koreans
are transparently boxed.

They smoke and eat and listen to
their everlasting gibberish,
the glossolalia of the world
that sounds like: You make a wish,
but reads — "Attendant has no cash."

They are forbearers and the guards
of morning yet to come.
At night these are the outposts
with the cigarettes and gum.

There nobody leaves a trace
when passing the vastness of
the black, suburban paradise
where the only light in the neighborhood
comes from a distant loft.

TOWN IN EUROPE

Craiova opens as you descend to the plains of hope
from red-stained peaks of Transylvania
at sunset. The trains leave for Bucharest, Vienna, through
the sunset of Europe to a comfortable oblivion of
golden age boyars, ladies in long embroidered dresses,
their necks desirable and vulnerable, the Hapsburg
smoldering decomposition beyond recognition. Traceable
light touch of the Ottoman ginger sweet suffocation
still lingers. Craiova: Brancusi gems stand silent
as professor Firan walks through the centuries'
watershed, a messenger of cultural genetic continuity.
21st Century percolates in smoky internet cafes,
decorated by assortment of Mirceas, Carmens and Sofias,
in short light skirts, their misty eyes give meaning
to interim existence, promising continuity for
the little dark-eyed boys, hopefully growing up safe
on the grassy wet meadows of Europe silent of horror.
Europe, almost gone, forgetting itself, ready for the next
fatal mistake of self-indulgence and reckless caution.
Craiova: a rare oasis, saving clear water of cultural memory,
old wine, dark grapes, fresh goat cheese, silver cups,
library in the dark silent stone building, not attended
any more by the coming generations clueless to
their own unknowable void.

SURF

The numbers repeat themselves
time and again, returning to a complete circle
of our lack of knowledge, back
to the graceful logic of long narrative.

We still try to penetrate
the very essence of this emanating,
impersonal, and centripetal passion,
as we live on the outskirts of the universe
on a clear night—lost, but not homesick—
hearing time moving, going nowhere
from nowhere.

Then one can see a family
by table light or by a bonfire,
the supper is over. They listen to verses
uttered in some language.
The original version is running
like shadow of a cloud
across the ruins of ancient city
by the seashore.

A man is standing there alone
all life long, counting
unending waves.

INCIDENTAL

They come in all colors
and shapes. I like them all
inadvertently, but it's eating me
all my life, piece by piece.
Left alone I know how indulging
thoughts of them might be and yet
I slowly move to the realization
of deep cleft between me and them.
And it's not just genetics, its
the free choice of the soul
in its slow motion
toward full buoyancy.
Thank God she also gets hungry
and thirsty and lets me go
on my own journey, while
she is not watching.
And then they come out
in all colors and shapes and
travel along in the empty air
of incidental encounters
only occasionally
leaving traces,
warm slender streams,
silver lining of misery
of incidental encounters.

HOLIDAY

From Bethlehem to the infirmary,
a convoy moved from the settlement
and was gone. The stony road was dark, and far
away the star of David shone solemnly.

By dawn the whole earth was covered
with salt as if by a dry hoarfrost.
Smoke stays in the valley. Grill is on.
The radar talks to a flying rocket.
Deep bottom of the cavern rots.
There sulfur in the hellfire smolders.

Church spire goes up to a bottomless void
and stands like a pinnacle of faith.
The feast is closer. Bazaar alive.
The priests are having tea, samovar puffs.
Some hug the sidewalk, some drink young wine
from a clay jug, yellow star rises.
That lonely string in the divan
still sings from the heaven, never silent.

The fires are on throughout the night,
and mist is settled on the harbor.
Northeast is blowing out of the void
over the hustle of brokers, clerks,
cathedrals, markets, tolls of warning.
And then the towers of Babel
are burning slowly in the morning.

SOUNDS OF NIGHT

Listen to the sounds of disappearance:
dog barking, piece of paper
with a handwritten note
burning in the fireplace,
telephone call unanswered,
answering machine broken,
can't find the second sock,
as the wife's blowing the horn outside,
while you're calling your mistress,
and you are set
to have a heart attack in the morning,
loving once, loving once
in a blue moon, as you feel
sweet inkling in Luna-park
close to the point of disembarkation,
where the stray submarine
washed up to the shore is turned
into a Russian restaurant.
There you sit and drink
to the blasting music
and sinking lights thinking
about what you have:
those heavy stocks of incidental life,
insuring a worthless thought of relief:
you never alone with yourself.
These are the sounds of disappearance:
wind slowing down,
tires on the gravel,
someone's black and white
school photograph at the roadside
yard sale. It stares at you
before you speed away,

disappearing from its life
and then end up
sitting in your own home,
looking at the framed face on the wall,
touched by a tender dust of an early Fall.

TRANSFER

Photo: bombed out Frankfurt,
backdrop on the wall of the Beerhalle.
Black and white photo
on the new gray grave stone.
Today the sky is a still bottom,
but no B-52 seen in the zone
of blown up sunset.
Here I am – only a shadow.
Random stop. Transfer
on the way from the past to faraway future.
What's left of the family tree –
foliage of letters, shadowless walls,
wooden bench overgrown with ivy
somewhere.
Day after tomorrow promises
calm and quiet. I do not believe
in its empty promises.
This place still is a smoky field,
smelling of death and soot.
The sky here is usually
cloudy velvet. We did not stay here for long.
Just black dots on white sheet of the landscape.
Black and white photo:
blown up Frankfurt.

III

PHOSPHENES

Today my beloved taught me a new unknown word – phosphenes.
Mysterious luminous floating stars, zigzags, swirls, spirals, appearing
        in the eyes without light
actually entering the eyes. For instance, if you press on your eyeballs.
The same effect may result from cosmic radiation. Neil Armstrong
        and other astronauts
experienced that on the cosmic orbit, when electromagnetic radiation
        from Earth was waning.
I understood that I see these phosphenes all my life: circles, labyrinth,
        DNA spirals. And they
actually smell: phosphorus, cosmos, unknown city, mountain road.
And I understood where the poems come from. They are kind of
        phosphenes.
You don't even have to close your eyes. You press on your internal eye
        and they appear.
And never vanish. Their appearance is inevitable, they don't
        disappear, and live inside you and
probably after you are gone.
Although I can't be sure about it, since I never lived after myself, after
        my own life.
At least so far.
But I seriously suspect that.
So, this is the danger to listen to your beloved. She also causes
        phosphenes to appear.
And then you can never escape.
I mean – escape phosphenes.

WARNING

Static and dead air
on incoming calls.
You will experience
silence while you waiting
for the next available
operator. Your call may be
monitored for quality
insurance purposes,
unless dead and static air
interferes with your
communication.
Anything incoming
may not be transmitted
due to current conditions.

In the meantime,
please, be aware
that proper entities
are working to restore
favorable conditions.
Be advised to be alert
and prepared to immediate
change of circumstances.
All assigned personnel
should remain at their
present locations and await
further instructions.
All non-essential personnel
should proceed to the designated
areas, avoiding static and dead air
at all costs.

AURORA BOREALIS

After watching plenty of Nordic TV series, we decided to travel and see aurora borealis with our own eyes. There, we booked the tour, and found ourselves in a cozy little cabin on themonstrous cruise ship. The porthole looking into the gray precipice of Northern seas. We were spending most of the time on the deck, watching skies gradually changing as we were moving to Arctic.

The fellow travelers would gather at the restaurant or on the deck. But as we approached North, the group would thin out. By Faroese Islands, most of the cabins were empty, dark, and from the ocean's abyss, our liner looked like huge half-abandoned building with rare lit windows in the wasteland of universe.

Then we were spending most of the time together alone. She wrapped up in her Scottish plaid, me with my cold cigar, watching darkening horizon, trying to catch a magic moment of the appearance of pale-pink aurora.

The tour booklets promised that on these altitudes, one can start seeing unearthly light.

Most common colors are pale rose or green. Blue or purple-red ones are very rare, and their nature is mysterious.

Eventually, we were alone on the deck, and as the ship was moving toward Northeast, we saw an unknown crimson light over Eurasia.

I hugged her shoulders and we descended into our cabin, into our world, or what was left of it.

As I looked into her eyes, I saw the same strange reflection of the faraway continent.

Then everything went out.

The black, unearthly wind was blowing by the side of the ship.

BREADCRUMBS

Breadcrumbs from breakfast,
cigarette stubs, bloody lipstick
on the coffee cup. That's what left.
Plus, remaining account with the health club,
now closed according to bankruptcy laws
in the state of New Jersey.
The gargantuan machines still there,
the dinosaurs' skeletons
in the Museum of Natural History.

Nothing natural
about the situation.
Just predestined tide of no luck,
almost rhymes with destination.
How simply and matter-of-factly
the whole tight unit
(me and her) would fall apart,
leaving on the floor
of now somebody else's home:
breadcrumbs from breakfast,
cigarette stubs, lipstick
on the coffee cup,
small amulet, bought together
in the Scola Spagnola in Venice
thousand years ago.

BORDER OF DREAM

She usually appears long before dawn.
Shadows live their own lives,
return to childhood comes momentarily,
and light is still very timid.
Her eyes are open but motionless,
and express something that is unreadable.
She comes very close and looks
through me to something far away and deep.
So unreachable, and I
would not even want to peer into it.
She probably knows something
that is unknowable to me,
and to no one, for that matter.
It is possible to follow her,
but the direction is unknown.
She goes slowly and her route is endless.
Sometimes she takes me for a flight.
I am slower, but she usually waits for me.
From the heights, I can see my hometown.
But now it's abandoned; nobody lives there anymore.
She usually promises something to me,
but never remembers her promises.
Her words of love live by themselves, unrelated to anyone.
Eventually she disappears, not remembering where she was.
She returns to that land, to that zone,
where light shadows are flowing
as on the surface of a mirror.
And afterward, everything is not what it appears to be,
and only light feeling of her breath on my cheek
tells me that she really was with me
telling me something important.
But what it was, I don't remember,
and it does not matter anyway,
since we conversed in nonexistent language.

BOY AND MOON

Sunrise over Nyack, son flows along Hudson
from North, from Labrador,
leaving behind Aurora Borealis.
It flows along farms and lakes, over sunset at Cape Cod,
along abandoned railroad tracks,
empty freight train cars.
Lights up dilapidated house by the road in Piermont,
over dark movie theater and desolate town, and turns
into moon. Lingers over Greenwich Village and descends
behind Hudson into green sponge of Jersey.
Boy wakes up from bad dream, turns around.
Empty, twilight, moon soundless.
"My God, what America did you have?
What happened to my home?"
No answer, and the boy falls asleep.

LIGHT YEAR

We are separated by light-years.
Meaning, I love turning on all the lights,
little lamps in corners, night table and all.
She likes twilight, or even darkness.
There is a smoldering conflict between us
related to closed, slightly open, or
completely closed blinds and curtains.
Still, at night, I like to home another nocturnal world—
float into darkness and to the place
where I am not visible.
She likes to lie down quietly, listen to her book,
or podcast on perfumes,
which is a black hole to me.
This is how we have lived and
loved each other and our light-years.
Late at night, it's all quiet,
and only police sirens far away,
fire engines, remind us that the other world exists.
Then they would disappear into the night.
And then she would listen to her Nordic noir and
I would listen to *Man Without Qualities* on my iPhone.
Screen would light up corners softly,
their shadowy life, hidden at daytime.
Never escaping completely.
I would get up, leave the phone at my night table,
frozen on a certain page.
And she would stay in bed, listening to her book
in the dusk-glow of my phone,
thinking that I am still there,
and not light-years away.

TRANSLINGUAL POETRY

Snuffbox. Aluminum from Messerschmitt.
Soldered red star of stained glass.
"To Coronel Ya.A.Gritsman from GIs of 222nd Division,
33d Red Army, 3d Belorussian Front, Western Region."
Location: Bookshelf Restoration Hardware,
Between Kafka and Celan.
A.Gritsman, M.D.
210 Riverside Drive, 7D
New York, NY 10025.
Rauchen nicht verboten

MARFA LIGHTS

Sad lights of Texas small towns.
Flickering souls of killed horsemen
on endless rootless prairie leading nowhere.
No man's land, black underground blood.

Texas towns: Marfa, Moscow, Odessa—
wild lights of distant names, flown from space
as seeds to the empty field.
I saw this flying 80 miles per hour on the road
to nowhere from nowhere.

Then planet Houston lit up on the horizon.
Wandering lights marked my back, and then
later that night in my dream, my father called.
I have not seen him for seven Soviet years after
my departure.

As I woke up, my father actually called,
and after all those years, I heard my own voice.
And he realized that was me—
his only son, born right after the war.
I have carried away this wandering light,
flickering between my scapulae.
And I am wondering what would happen
with that light when I am no more.

SUBURBAN HAPPINESS

God, I'd like to start all over again!
Get settled in the suburban home, surrounded
by magnolias and rickety fence.
Take out trash on Wednesdays,
Recycling on Thursdays.
Coming home on time.
Tell you about days' events.
Take off my tie, looking carnivorously
at your turkey cutlets.
Smoke quietly, watching as you
go meticulously through days' mail.
Watch my TV series half-heartedly.
By midnight, go to bed,
read some of Kafka's diaries,
look through last *New Yorker* poems
that remind me of boat frames
on the banks of dried-out lakes.

To feel the happiness of this
inhabited island in the ocean of life.
Wait for the moment of your light,
feminine sleep, floating
further and further from me
to the shores of your girlhood.

Then seize the moment,
get out of bed,
break out soundlessly,
the door of our refuge,
jump outside and run
where the eyes look.
Passing somebody else's
phosphorescent windows,
leaving shreds of skin on the branches.

Reach wet ravine on the outskirts.
Where fire is still smoldering,
Smoke of some tree unknown to me.
Find that spot where I once hid something
I can't find.
Notice the light shadow of her figure
Vanishing into bushes.

STREET

I remember the stone wall along the street and smoke over the invisible river.
I am one of them, but my presence of unknowable to them and still
I am one of the shadows on the wall
calling, stretching my hand but one cannot cross that street.
This twilight world is quiet, no sound. The shadows on the wall vanished without a trace. The memory of stone akin the ivy crawling, mycelium of memory, cemetery thicket. But the dispute is meaningless: hand doesn't reach the birds flown away. The gate's ajar. But no people, no faces.

And yet everything shows that the life has existed and still exists. As if almighty passed by touching with his wing night shadow of the tower. His trace has disappeared.
But on the street, those two figures continue their endless discourse.
And they don't hear him.
He lives in the noise of lindens and in the touch of wind from invisible fields beyond the city.

Somewhere nearby the child is not asleep. He hears the hubbub of adults and then it's a quiet hour. One cannot hear the sound of bodies but only whisper of the souls along the street.
Where an angel has just flown by.
There is no exit, but it's not a dead end. The boundaries of the city lie in the unconsciousness of fields. There is still light.

Transparent early evening. It's time to go home – toward the light, toward smell of life. But there is no place to go. Last trace is cold. The disposition of bodies, geometry of gesture – along the Lobachevski lines along the haze beyond the horizon.

But there is no horizon. There is only street as a line of the lost names of last words – an immeasurable remainder of the unsaid. Then figures are melting and the speech disappears in the forest. And who knows if birds have souls or it's only a clot of the smooth musculature harboring its tart gulp.

Still, places have souls. Thus irradiated forest carries its destiny through nuclear ravine. The street almost empty, dust, rustle of fate. Although there is no promise that anybody will reach his destination.

An in the morning there is no coins left, no things dropped in the twilight by the stone gates. Nobody will come. Beyond the window life is silent like a still life, unmovable until next century. There is thin pulse – life on a thin thread. Light of the dark eyes in the gloomy dilution of the darkness.

That's how my family is: everyone scattered. The molecules of love dissipated around the world, and on the way there I am talking to myself, but woman – fate would listen for a moment, nod and then slowly leaves along this quiet street beyond the frame without an answer.

WILDERNESS

Three hundred yards from a ranger station by the Pacific Highway, our footprints wane as we walk on the thick duff teeming with insects. A lonely lightning, quick wildfire, and the smoldering burning leave melting patches on the dark forest floor and "goose pens" on the trunks.

A natural wooden cave inside a tree is carved gradually during two or three centuries—formerly, a shelter for an emaciated escapee from the mission, skinning a raccoon, listening to the ringtail cats which rustle in the bushes. Nowadays, it makes a cover for a gray-braided hippie, nursing his last joint, watching a mountain lion creeping after its prey or for a tired hiker, listening to a heavy rain outside.

In the canyons and on the flats beside the river, sycamores marry the black cottonwoods, big-leaf maples, alders, and willows. As they migrate to the south-facing slopes they give way to the chaparrals, shrubs of chamise, manzanita, and yucca. The ravines are overgrown with oaks, tan oaks, and laurels.

The cliffs remain calm, witnesses of so many ships sunk so close to their destination. At the promontory they hold the pulsating lonely eye of the lighthouse, being rather a memory monument than a real path to salvation. The masts of the redwoods, the tallest and some of the oldest living organisms on earth, shield the vast approaches to a hilly terrain and to the valley entrances standing on eternal guard even before God was born, when only his soul was listening in its sleep to a primordial song of the trees' tidal breathing.

UNTITLED

Residual air motionless
in the cervices of an anonymous
forest. The road to the abandoned station
is short. Departure unknown.
I figured the rest of the road,
touched the papers in my pocket.
Moon lit up the escape route for a moment
and then drowned like a coin
of the distant land.
Waiting at the platform
I looked at the photo
in unsure light: there
are dear faces with
a fleeting touch of happiness
already fading away
in the smoky haze
of the departure.

IV

FIRST MEMORY

My first memory was that I was playing a tiger,
a happy baby tiger,
my mom threw me an apple, laughing, beaming.
That was before her hypertension,
before the magnesium in a tightly curtained room,
before Grandma's stroke on a hot July day at the dacha,
at the strawberry patch,

before my father's tenure as a labor
camp physician at the Great Kara-Kum Canal,
when I forgot how he looked.
Before the City of Kalinin on the dead frozen Volga,
Eastern pagan winds blowing from a thousand years ago.

That was before my blood on the Caucasian glacier,
live dark spot going down into the time crevice,
before The Hard Days Night in 1968 Prague

and before Mom was crawling on her knees
as Dad was shutting the family door one cold early spring.
This is before I saw the spotted white planes of the Middle-
        Russian Elevation
through Aeroflot illuminator, sipping cheap soviet champagne,
my eyes dry from exertion.

That was before I left home for good
and bad and you turned in your bed and met the eyes
of the white wall.

That was before the edge of Newark, her walker,
the SSI, pellet bullet missing my head,
smashing the rear window,
before her slurred speech and semi-oblivion.
That was before,
that was before my memory...

DON'T LOOK BACK

Don't even talk about returning.
The past becomes
a worn-out coin,
preserve gone sour.
You learn signs of the departure:
train car moving nowhere,
airport terminal – silent octopus,
muffler's machine gun series,
smoke over trembling road,
still life of abandoned family
table with a lone pear on it.
If you close your eyes
you find yourself
among mirror images
of your family portrait.
Then you understand –
you are already there,
just a flicker
in the morning reflection.

DOUBLE

I spent my life in struggle with you.
All my life since I was standing on the sidewalk
by my dear old home,
covered by frozen vapor.
And now I linger
with my head down
listen to what my onlooker
whispers to me
There is no answer
to those questions of youth,
and as I fall asleep dawn flows in
and plugs my ears
with the dead cotton balls
of denial.
Forgive me please, I dare no evil,
but still my lost head
falls into my empty hands,
which cannot hold a book.
But my light words
sparkle through darkness
flying into the world
to nowhere.
And he, my friend, my interlocutor
sits in front of me, thoughtful and gray-haired,
silent, smoking nervously, my old pal.
Dead phone stores empty promises.
But there was a third one, impeccable,
focused, but went unnoticed by him and by me
and passed by us
as a transparent shadow.

VILLA BORGHESE

As you leave the place,
leaves fall down;
sundown lingers,
and then it is gone.

The place stays still
as time passes,
unnoticed by anyone
but you.

Then someone else comes,
looks at the sunset,
drops a cigarette stub
into dry foliage,
a paper napkin, a note
on someone's card.
Then he goes too,
on his way around the circle.

You remember that
bittersweet, warm smell
of magnolias, maple,
the rustle of the cracked fountain.
Late sun touches
the statue with its disfigured,
unrecognizable face.
You are calm and happy
for the moment.

The salvation is that
you could not even know:
You were not the only one there

ACKNOWLEDGEMENTS

Thanks to the editors of following publications in which these poems first appeared, sometimes in a slightly different form:

Hawaii Review: Christmas Poem (Holiday)
Gloom Cupboard: Dead Air
OPEN: Journal for Arts and Letters: Empty House by Hudson, German Rug, Two Planes
Carbon Culture Review: Escape, Last Words
Lips: Farewell
Slant: A Journal of Poetry: First Memory, Metro-North
Tampa Review: Forget the Wedding
Foliate Oak: Hudson River (Hudson)
El Portal: Light in the Cathedral
Midwest Quarterly: Moscow Walk
Seattle Star: N.J. State Highway, Bust
Vita Brevis: Night Watchman
Schuylkill Valley Journal of Arts: Pacific Highway (Wilderness)
Steam Ticket: Siege of Moscow
Litbreak Magazine: Street
Alembic: Transfer
Forge Journal: Unborn (Crossing the Line)
Verdad: Unsheltering Sky
Courtship of Winds: Villa Borghese
The Magnolia Review: Warning, Colosseum
HOBART: White Lies
I-70 magazine: Light Year
Best American Poetry Blog: 5 ADAR II 5771
Cerasus Magazine (North London): Marfa Lights
SLAB: Rain Jazz
South Florida Poetry Journal: The Motel

AFTERWORD

Andrey Gritsman is one of those rare souls who can exist as a poet in more than one language with clarity, precision and music. How does he do it? In his native Russian he has a supreme command of form, his poems are so musical you remember the whole stanzas even if you read them just once. In English, as with the book you are holding in your hands, he is able to give us something new: a directness of tone that is nevertheless mysterious.

But we just jumped the train
ahead of schedule, on time,
in the only destined station,
in our case paradoxically set
in the midst of the imperial,
pompous, dead exuberance.

In both languages he is the master of elegiac tone, his poetics explore meanings and mysteries of human memory. But here, in *Crossing Lines*, I also get a sense of clarity, as if one is writing about final things, as if the perspective of a foreign language gives one a distance that allows to see things with precision that is almost eerie. Yes there isn't just a welcome strangeness here (as is often the case with writers who work in a foreign language), there is also a kind of wisdom with comes from the experience of crossing that line:

I live my life by white lies.
And poetry is white lies.
Second language is white lies also.
As well as the first.

But language is the only way
to hide love.
White, black, transparent
Or otherwise invisible.
So, all day long,
All life long I say white lies
To hide my love. In fact
I never know to whom.

I sense there is something almost Borgesian here, but without
the fiction element, it puts me in the mind of late Mark Strand's
final poems, perhaps, but there is a distinct Eastern European
atmosphere (that Moscow Presnya subway station, that
Georgian eatery, those dumplings, of course, and vodka, yes; but
it is the metaphysics that make the atmosphere genuine)—

Steel light in the morning
hint of moss in the air.
Smell of distant fisheries
abandoned.
Seven potato dishes on the menu.
All is not what it seems.

Perhaps the mystery I sense here is the mystery one senses in
the love lyrics of poets who write in their later years, when the
romanticism gives a way to philosophical questions of what
it might mean to love, what might it mean to be: the poem's
speaker becomes that "traveler" who knows that "his death /
became new language / poetry turned / into palpable matter."

The air itself. Air, in fact, is a frequent actor in these poems. There was a hint of moss in the air in the lyric I just mentioned. And now we are given a lyric where the poet takes the bureaucratic language of answering machine, plus a bit of air, to make something entirely new, and eerie, happen:

Your call may be
monitored for quality
assurance purposes,
unless dead and static air
interferes
[...]All nonessential personnel
should proceed to the designated
areas, avoiding static and dead air
at all costs.

This is a poet who isn't interested in patronizing us, or glazing over, he tells it like it is, and if his tone is sober, at least we know we are looking with clarity either at the present moment or at the past. But even if we are looking at the photo of bombed out city (as in a moving poem, Transfer) there is clarity that is strangely affirming in its starkness. But in the directness, beauty also resides: "There hangs above the parking lot / the lunar, dim eyeball" he says, and "gas stations" are "nests / of alienated warmth." Beauty also resides in the mysterious. When the poet's beloved teaches him "a new unknown word— phosphenes" we are given to see how the stars are entering the eyes. And with revelation, wisdom comes:

I understood that I see these phosphenes all my life: circles, labyrinth, DNA spirals. And they actually smell: phosphorus, cosmos, unknown city, mountain road.And I understood where the poems come from. They are kind of phosphenes.

You don't even have to close your eyes.

Indeed. Crossing the Line is an honest book something one can't always say about poetry collections, it is one man's spiritual search into daily mysteries around how, however stark or terrifying these daily facts might be. In these times we need all the mystery we can get in order to learn, when time comes, to cross the line. May this collection find many readers.

Ilya Kaminsky

ABOUT THE AUTHOR

Andrey Gritsman, came to the US from Russia in 1981. He is a physician, poet and essayist, writes in two languages. He has been nominated for the Pushcart Prize several times and shortlisted for PSA Poetry Prize. Poems, essays, and short stories have appeared in many journals including *New Orleans Review, Notre Dame Review, and Denver Quarterly*, anthologized and translated into several European languages. He authored fifteen books of poetry and prose in both languages. He edits international poetry magazine *Interpoezia* (www.interpoezia.org).

Previous collections from *Cervena Barva Press: Live Lanscape* and *Family Chronicles*.

www.andreygritsman.com

www.ingramcontent.com/pod-product-compliance
Lightning Source LLC
Chambersburg PA
CBHW020214090426
42734CB00008B/1073